There's a worldliness world-weariness, in fact, the opposite: there's a joy in experience, an experience that has given birth to wisdom, a wisdom that is neither heavy nor ponderous, but an intelligence that shares its discoveries lightly, invitingly, which is what makes this collection so captivating, and the poet such good company. It is rare for a first book to have such range and depth —the trials of the immigrant; the paradoxes of romance and family life; the wrangling with saints as well as sinners—*So Long the Sky* is a beautifully written travelogue of the soul.

— John Skoyles, author of *The Nut File* and *Inside Job*

Centuries. Countries. Canaries. These words echo back to me when I put down *So Long the Sky* and go out into the day. The poems in Mary Kovaleski Byrnes' collection span the world, from Pennsylvania to Russia and back. But also, like rivers becoming seas becoming rivers again, these poems span that great curving gulf between desire and acceptance, between ruin and forgiveness. She writes, "these things I try to name each day / were never mine to lose," and I am struck with how, even in this space of loss, Byrnes has created such vast tributaries of meaning. Yes, we sin every hour of every day. But, as Byrnes writes, our faces "will turn / as foreign as a century." We continue, forever in the process of becoming. These poems are blessed with life and change. Like birds, these poems move from ash to flame and then back to life. They are a reaching-back and a reaching-toward. They are the key in the lock, the door opening, and that hope, that hope, that hope, that everything will return, as you have, despite so much, to this place of love. Yes, I love this book.

— Devin Kelly, author of *In This Quiet Church of Night, I Say Amen*

Mary Kovaleski Byrnes' rich first collection, *So Long the Sky*, roots us in a particularly American past: "city bus, wet woolen coat," "pork and sauerkraut for luck." With humor and insight, in inventive forms and varied tones, Byrnes gives us all of "*hard coal*" "Coal Country," its joys and tragedies: "Yes, the fire's still going. / Yes, they left the old country for this." We can see ourselves in our grandparents' immigrant pasts, and in "boats brimming with refugees" in water that "spit a toddler out on a beach." These poems see home so clearly they break down distinctions between citizen and refugee, plead with us to define family more widely: "No borders / No borders / No borders."

— Jill McDonough, author of *Reaper* and *Where You Live*

So Long the Sky

MARY KOVALESKI BYRNES

Mary Kovaleski Byrnes

*For Isabela,
with gratitude &
admiration
— MKB.*

PLATYPUS PRESS, England

Copyright 2018 by Mary Kovaleski Byrnes
All rights reserved.

Excerpt from "Sleep", from Ploughshares Fall 2011 issue, by Alan Williamson. Copyright 2011 by Alan Williamson. Used by permission of Ploughshares at Emerson College.
Text for "Centralia Mine Fire Project: History and Recommendations for Control" taken from *Fire Underground: The Ongoing Tragedy of the Centralia Mine Fire*. Copyright 2010 by David DeKok. Used by permission of Globe Pequot Press.
The title of "Whatever We Name, We Exceed" is a line from Eleanor Rand Wilner, "Interview" from *The Girl With Bees in Her Hair*. Copyright 2004 by Eleanor Rand Wilner. Used with the permission of The Permissions Company, Inc., on behalf of the author and Copper Canyon Press, coppercanyonpress.org.

ISBN 978-1-9997736-7-0

First Edition, 2018

Cover and interior layout by Peter Barnfather
Cover photography by Stte Funn
Type set in Bergamo Pro, FontSite Inc.
Printed and bound by Clays Ltd, Elcograf S.p.A.

Published by Platypus Press

10 9 8 7 6 5 4 3

for my family

1. Centralia

   I.

5. Whistling Language
7. Always, Ditto
9. X, 1926
11. Upon Finding St. Bernadette without Her Hands
13. St. Edith of Centralia
15. Porch Talk
17. A Photo of Poland in Pennsylvania
18. How to Collect Coal from a Moving Train
20. Looking at the American Girls
    in Club Y2K, Gdansk
23. Reading Anna Karenina
    at the Susquehanna Valley Mall
25. Maybe This Happens to Everyone
27. Aubade with Accident

   II.

33. Black Sea
35. For Work
38. Rositsa in Love in English (i)
39. To My Polish Aunts
41. Postcards, Bulgaria
44. Haikus: Rositsa's Luggage
45. Ricky's Back from Iraq

47. Valentine's Day, Manhattan
49. Commonwealth
51. Kowalewski vs.

III.

57. Alternate Invitations to a Meteor Shower
59. Aubade: To Each His Dulcinea
60. Level, madam, level.
62. Half Orange
64. 11:59 p.m.
66. Confessional
68. A Photo of Pennsylvania in Fiji
69. The Other Side of Water
71. There, There Catastrophe
73. Centralia Mine Fire Project: History
      and Recommendations for Control
74. Triptych with Excerpt from
      Coal Miner's Industrial Handbook
75. Coal Country, with Anniversary
77. The Floating Island

IV.

83. Limbic Morning
85. Rositsa at the Communist Monument
88. Limbo
90. The Road to Fethiye

92.	Poem with So Many Bodies in It
94.	Rositsa in Love in English (ii)
96.	At the Mall with the Anthracite Queens
99.	Rositsa in Love in English (iii)
101.	If You Wonder Why the River
102.	A Wedding in Poland
104.	Whatever We Name, We Exceed
106.	Volcano with Child

109.	Thanks
110.	Acknowledgements & Notes
111.	About the Author

CENTRALIA

How does an inferno begin?
    Let me guide your hands
        on the wheel. Drive us toward the ruin.

The birches' new green
    on jet-black culm and Good Friday threatening
        snow. This town's a funeral

pyre. Blocks of houses boarded,
    save one.
        They dug coal holes in the cellar,

called it *robbing back*. But didn't a thousand men get left
    with shovels in their hands?
        This land's a wreck.

I promise you, it was not ignorance, only love
    and hunger. And fire
        will only travel

where it can breathe. We are
    midway, the first stations of suffering.
        We don't have to kiss

the stigmata for another three hours.
    We could drive to the place where everything started.
        It's ours, after all—

this empty time.

I.

WHISTLING LANGUAGE

It's last night again. Sky lit up
from another eon. Airplane pushing east

over the Pacific, a belly full of televisions.
The children fashion paper bag wings, jump off

the shed into the rhododendrons. Still, we dream
embraces with the gone-before. The never-been.

A doorway in an upside-down world—
a childhood home afloat on a raging sea.

I'll soar across it, only to land once more
on that autumn road by the coal slag mountain,

leaves singing by our ears, a voice
I love and lose again on waking.

Someday, I promise, we'll go to La Gomera,
where the people have learned to be birds.

We'll circle the volcano, listening.
Soon enough, a call from one coffee-ground hill

to another. The whistling language—
lilt and grammar transcribed

into the ancient mimicry of canaries.
We'll hear them, but won't understand the message

from shepherd to shepherd across the divide:
I've lost one down the hill. If someone's up there,

tell me, what can you see?

ALWAYS, DITTO

We spent the evening naming imaginary babies.
When I called one *Natalie*, she suddenly grew
a face. I called her before, in a forest of boats,

and found her, floating on an island
in a book under glass. For decades,
they asked questions there, recorded people—

books as tired as diaspora's exhale, a thousand *Natalies*,
a million first words. Mothers try to preserve them
but they'll age and warp no matter: the box of footprints,

fabled alligator, broken teeth. I was named
for a woman who crossed an ocean,
who would not remember the scale of green waves—

everything before this was destroyed.
Words blown to the currents,
words out the bomb bay doors.

Natalie. Ruthenian—the island book told me
all it knew. A crude label for skin,
for religion. Distance, a kept illusion.

How long does the alien wish to remain in America?
Always. Her answer the same as the others
in an officer's shorthand—*Ditto*.

A thousand pages of *aliens*, a history
of *ditto*. All we've lost in the naming,
between the ordered ledger lines they drew.

X, 1926

His hand on her housedress
and men at the door.

What holds a place in history
for the illiterate? The muted immigrant?

The woman who just wanted
children and quiet? She'll never

pass down this violence.
Better even to change dates

on graves. What flight
looks like when you have no fists

and only love: years on the phone
to get the black lung money. Crash

of a wrecking ball next door.
Whatever you do, don't

say his name. Let him
die already. *Good riddance.*

Don't stick around for the bulldozers
coming over the hill. I thought I heard them

but maybe you were just shaking
down the stove. I want to apologize—

I think I've remembered
all the wrong things.

On the census, her signature,
her hand writing the children's names,

his. She hands over
the pen. He leaves an X.

UPON FINDING ST. BERNADETTE WITHOUT HER HANDS

(If we're going to erase ourselves
    which selves
        which parts)

I held a fragment
    bone, or stone, or
        (something
            off

in my childhood) a stone
    finger or
        nose

Once, votives glimmered like confetti
    (and can't burn
        a prayer up)

They say the missing
    girl dropped her backpack in the creek
        A warning with

leeches
    We are just girls
        (or was it torn from her)

            rose-petal rosaries
ring around—running
      tearing at our legs
           red welts, red clots (a pox, a mystery)—what else
               could those old nuns tell us

How to explain
      a hammer to the chin
           (of a blessed woman frozen)
           a pink backpack
                 (in the creek)

What hands will be stone
      (on our bodies)
           There are soldiers nearby
      they are always drilling
           in our schoolyard

The boys play (army)
      in the trees
      the girls must leave
(our offerings)
      at the feet of something
           not quite whole

ST. EDITH OF CENTRALIA

after Wisława Szymborska & Natalie Diaz

Left when her mother's house was condemned
to live in Manayunk, cut hair with Pina,
marry Lon. Thick plastic on their mauve sofa, the good
one. A laugh like a jackhammer, five nights a week
at the polka club, and everyone knows
she's always dancing. Like that, the years:
Dancing. Laughing. Cutting hair.
Ukie-Jersey cranberry beehive,
made possible by six decades
of Aquanet. The warning on the hot pink
can: EXTREMELY FLAMMABLE.
She keeps clear of fires
of all sorts—birthday cakes carried
like pin-pulled grenades, baptismal
candles snuffed out
as soon as they sent the demons off on their dark-angel
express-chariot to hell. Lon always said
they'd go home, especially after
the stillborn, the first
born. A cold hospital
on a Florida morning. Her honeymoon.
Novena every Monday, forty years
at Holy Family. Said they'd go back
after the fires went out.
Manayunk stuck in her throat
each time she wrote home. No people
like her people. Yes, she looked
back. Every time. A Sodom, for certain:
mother at the Geisinger choking

on cancer, step-father trying to claw his chest open
on the living room floor, sister's eyes—
bit-coaled, opiate-gone, until she disappeared
with a migrant. So many Vets lost
at the Ukrainian Club. And then, a newborn
wrapped tight and frost-still
in a hospital-provided blanket and hat. Photographs
line the Manayunk staircase, each one
of home, each one an image of smoke.
Salt on the steps for snow like shattered teeth,
none in the food since Lon's triple bypass, so Sunday
dinner's bland, the living
son, gone, and married
a woman named Charity and then a woman named Taylor.
The son, Taylor, Taylor's mother, her four kids, two Chihuahuas—
the lot of them rootless, listless,
always on the move to a new
McMansion loaded
with plastic Kalashnikovs and ash-haired, broken-armed princesses,
and once, a salt water pool out back.
Slick anthracite color.
The water hard, soft. Her son saying,
*Why are you so hung up on that
shit-town.* And, *Mom, get in the pool already*.
Taylor shoveling deviled
eggs in her face as if
the apocalypse was nigh. Lon driving home on 76, hands tight
on the wheel, Edith's skin itchy, a snake's, trying to shed,
or a bride's, laced white.

PORCH TALK

Let's play football again,
grass stain my Easter tights, chase
the wild alley dogs.
The cousins from Jersey won't.
We're better than them.
I'm them and I'm not.

Let's get lost in the pickle maze
in the basement. In the jars' murky
wombs a thousand embryos
will survive another winter.

I've picked you
for this. We'll tour
the mines together.
But wait, I'm still

with the other
children on the porch swing
afraid of the Doberman
next door. *the doors
the doors the doors.*

We're gathering our history
in dropped sentences
that sound like Ukrainian
Jesus. We won't ask—
cancer, stripper, bedroom

door. When we get bored,
we beg them to take us to see
the town on fire.

A PHOTO OF POLAND IN PENNSYLVANIA

   after Richard Hugo

Afternoon, hot air balloons over cornfields,
the sky aflame with patchwork suns.

You're on the porch swing,
stripping snap peas. Your daughter, bruised

and quiet in the yard.
Your hands were never anything

but thick and dark from work. *Where did you take
the cow?* You ask the children. *We have only her milk*

and the cucumbers. The children have gone
chasing balloons. They want to touch the fiery hearts.

*Listen, tanks are coming up the street. They'll steal
our sons for good. They'll drop them*

*from the sky into another country. A different country.
It couldn't have been the one we left.* But look—

> the children there know how to sniff the air, then climb
> the honeycomb cliffs. How the sea

> hides the cove and then bares
> its curve at low tide. Look

> at the women's faces, the shape
> of their brows. They're yours. They're mine.

HOW TO COLLECT COAL FROM A MOVING TRAIN

While you wait for the whistle, place a penny
    on the track. Count the cars
        when they blur by, the coal as it flies

out like popcorn. Scramble faster
    than the other children—a skirtful can heat
        even the flimsiest structure, will make you dream

of islands. From the air over Boston, you can almost touch them.
    On each descent, I number their backs,
        even the rocks jutting high and lonely,

wishing again for an era of shipwrecks.
    For the fogged-out survivors, those rocks
        would have been land enough for a hard-scrabble home.

My grandmother made her own rock, her own decades
    of lost ships. Slept seven siblings under coats in one bed,
        tells me how to collect coal

from a moving train, how to replace its dust with rain.
    At her sister's funeral, she shows me how every woman
        is a swallowed canary.

I forgot this, and the requiem's chorus,
    how the scapular itched my neck,
        even the story of the boy who stood too close

to the penny when the locomotive made it a flat bullet,
    drove it right through him.
        From the side of the highway in another country,

I watch the jacaranda spew its brilliance: paper-fire floating
    in all that hot steel. I have no place
        being here—this sudden knowledge

twisted copper in my chest. An immigrant man
    walks back and forth when the light turns red,
        selling packets of tissues.

He says, *Please, lady, you need these,*
    the birds around here
        make foreigners sneeze.

LOOKING AT THE AMERICAN GIRLS
IN CLUB Y2K, GDANSK

If the newest theory is
that there are eleven Americas,
you were in the sweet nothings,
a still life
with locusts, strobe lights,
and a warning
of weather.

It's fair to say we had something
      in common. Arrogance
           wobbling, those strange minutes
in the early aughts—
      curtain of invincible ideals
           fallen like the shot-down birds you were,
   young
      limbs swaying in time
           to an excuse for
   music.

Moments ago the planes were re-purposed.

The Americans on the dance floor love Tupac
Until the End of Time. The Israeli soldiers buy another
round—bump to your grind.

Weapons of mass destruction abstract
on the bar's television
but they're growing
untended in the corners of your imagination.

We had something in common:
Under an upside-down sky you dream of
future babies. Their skin, like yours, night visions.

You are one body, divisible—
        more energy of heart than
              gut, the only things
moving. Impossible savior,
        instinct and rhythm, never
              innuendo.

You blather about nation
building to a solidarity
of shipbuilders' sons.
        It keeps you
safe and ignorant, this America:
Connecticut's ease, Pennsylvania's blank face,
or the space you need
to be wild, flat and empty,
bored buffalo on the prairie.

Let's start over, where there's nothing to do,
where the snow's to the roofline,
and it's calling for more.

The trail has been buried long enough
for another coalition of the willing.
We can count our blessings
between tornadoes.

READING ANNA KARENINA
AT THE SUSQUEHANNA VALLEY MALL

Tolstoy was born for this—
so a young girl can fall in love
reading on a bench at the shopping plaza.
Behind her, the army
recruitment booth fires off another round
of Neil Diamond. He sings *America*—
its endless fill-in-the-blanks. The incredulity
of bookstore and army, Target and Denny's
all shined up and stacked together,
the clean, smooth empire of pavement conquering
the old country back-break, plough and drought.
Cars warm and purring in the parking lot.
No more sardine-can train economy,
their dim-lit compartments where Anna waits
wearing *that* coat. The wool and fur collar
all the Russian heroines have—
the kind of coat your mother wore
in the '70s, when she fell in love
with your father and chose between milk
and bread at the Acme, and knew
the kind of happiness only Russian heroines know.
She wrote about it in a letter
for you to find in a shoebox under the stairs,
decades later, the beam of the flashlight
like a train cutting the forests
outside St. Petersburg, scanning her handwriting
in that damp space where you used to go
to read smutty novels, to learn what men do
with their calloused hands.

How there's never time
for buttons. And how women's shirts can burst open
like flocks of pigeons tearing from a belfry,
their bodies exploding,
like tanks in the desert, lined up
and firing,
so loud the soldiers crouch behind them,
mouth words to prayers or recite the names
of all the girls they ever touched—
the best friend, the best
friend's girl, the wife, the prom date,
Ashley, Jessi, Crystal, Maria—
as they shatter the world around them
and cover their heads with their hands.

MAYBE THIS HAPPENS TO EVERYONE

When I woke, Paris was in flames.
I spent the day in bed while a man I loved
kissed my ankles, the white arches
of my feet, asked what made them.
I told him it was the Sacré Cœur;
when a city is burning there's no time
for lies. At night the flames were in my hair,
the flames were in his mouth and each street
unrolled like a long tongue that gave
us what we couldn't understand.
If we'd danced on the cobbles
they'd have lit up like the disco floors
of Les Grands, like the smooth-trodden
gravestones of popes inside the cathedral,
the martyrs emblazoned on the Bastille.
It is impossible to remember
when his hand is up my dress on the metro
and Paris is in flames. The trains
brought us in through a tunnel underwater:
a tunnel made of glass,
the train, like a chain of dolphins linked end to end,
arching silver with the currents.
We saw Humpbacks, eyes as big as our train car,
slow and bovine—it took minutes to pass them.
Their whale eyes were looking at us—
everyone in Paris was looking at us.
We weren't looking at anyone, and when we did
their faces were like mirrors, I loved
his strange watery reflections but kissed only him.

The trains came. The trains moved out
of the blue-glass station while we ate crêpes
and called them *crapes* because we're American.
The trains came. We stayed. We were so young,
our hearts like Molotov cocktails,
like stones through leaded window glass.
Maybe this was the beginning of the world again, maybe
it was the end—maybe this happens to everyone
in every city, even in small towns, where corn fields
catch fire at the end of summer
and teenagers tear off their clothes
and run naked, tempting
the flames with their flawless skin.
It won't brand them, won't even singe them,
no matter how hard they run.

AUBADE WITH ACCIDENT

It didn't take much
to rattle our small world

with its dependable sun,
and the people we knew.

When we woke in our beds
the sky was gone, obliterated

in humid August fog.
We went walking anyway.

Heart Pine barn hulking
over our shoulders.

The mist, a bell-mute, deadened
what we might have said.

The sudden appearance of horses,
shag-maned, enormous teeth,

amuck in the tobacco field.
A break in the fence—

sharp tangle of wire and wood. Tire-rut.
Milkweed and cocklebur pillaged.

Quiet there, except the distant engine
of a biplane, the swoop of whippoorwill.

What we'd learn was saved
from us for then, as we looked up

to a silver wing,
felt the cool relief of rain.

II.

BLACK SEA

When Borislav tells me to eat the fish,
slender silver finger, head still on,
fried to a crisp, I do. This is how older men
spend late afternoons:
coffee, rakia, eggplant, smelts.
They eye my foreign face.
The Black Sea will find its bed barren today,
nothing to toss on the beach.
In the distance, a barge moves toward port,
blares *Москва* in red Cyrillic.

Kaloyan joins us, sports Oakley sunglasses
bought four years ago in Virginia with American dollars
earned slopping remains
of prime rib and tiramisu at the sink
of a casino's restaurant. Our talk turns
to the sea, its waters anoxic, breathless,
and all they touch—rotten undercurrent
of black market slave trade, young girls
hustled from Georgia's villages
to the brothels of Turkey.

We stay into the night, then find a bar,
a chalga band, violin ripping through the ancient
walls of what was once catacombs,
then wine cellar, then prison.
Now all its secrets are revealed in the singer's voice,

the loss and pain of generations, the honey
of her low notes so beautiful
for a moment we forget, breathe deep the thick air,
turn to each other, touch glasses, dance.

FOR WORK

In Moscow, I am asked to state my intentions.
The immigration officer's voice so Boris-and-Natasha,
I want her to say
moose and squirrel, moose and squirrel, is always
moose and squirrel. Not a chance—
her disdain for me warranted. I don't know anything—
my knowledge of this country: Saturday morning
cartoons, passed-down grudges,
and a typography of snow. *I'm here*
for work, I say. Unprepared, impractical
coat. It's too cold in this arrivals hall,
she's wearing woolen gloves with the fingers cut off.
I've brought in the last gulp of frigid air.
I've drunk too much vodka.
Didn't sleep, just read
Anna Karenina all the way from JFK,
same as the woman next to me,
going to see her grandmother one more time
before she dies, in Krasnodar. Then to Israel to do IVF cheaper—
so brave this woman with the simultaneous death and life
waning and unfurling outside and within her, flying
countless miles to lie in a hospital,
her legs in the stirrups of her mother country,
let the doctor take her eggs,
put a baby back in.
In Moscow I ask
hundreds of students to state their intentions.
Why do you want to work in the United States?

Why will you be a good dishwasher?
I don't know anything
about dishwashing. We meet in the Palace
of Culture and Sports. I'm 24.
They're 24. 21. 19. I have pee on my shoes—
the bathroom a porcelain hole in the floor
and I've used it backwards. A rusted cosmonaut
stalled on the lawn—a long-ago promise
to take their fathers and mothers way further
than dumb, capitalist America, all the way to outer space. In the hotel
they've spelled my name the Russian way.
Welcome, Mr. Kovalevsky, the TV says. The TV thinks
I'm a Russian man. My grandfather said, *We're not Russians.
Polish. Don't ever say Russian.* And my grandmother
on the other side, insisted, *Ukrainian. Catholic. Never
Russian.* When the DNA test says *Ashkenazi*,
she says, *Not surprised*.
She asks, *Why would you want
to go back there?* Her knowledge, a passed-down
fragment of secrets, identities denied.
The work they did to distance themselves
from this part of the world—
house cleaner, coal miner, snow plower—
the kinds of work you do when you've forgotten
yourself long ago, think instead of the next generation,
consume whole the idea
of America, the idea of the descendant
who'll grow up with time

to learn the xylophone, to major
in an impractical subject in a leafy college,
and how someday she'll be the first one
to go back, to Poland, Ukraine, even Russia,
the first one to put her feet
on the shitty ruts of a porcelain hole
in the floor, to think it funny, this hole in the floor,
funny too, the pee on her shoes, funny the immigration woman
with her prim hair, her red red lipstick, her funny, stereotypical meanness.
Your granddaughter, the first one
to get the resonant stamp IN without trying, shoves that blue
passport privilege in her back pocket, walks through
the narrow gate, not knowing what to expect on the other side,
feeling not fear but wonder, and the air so cold in her nose—
it stings her eyes, makes them tear.

ROSITSA IN LOVE IN ENGLISH (i)

at the deep of her / generator hum comfort / Plovdiv's cinderblock towers / his violin / all night / now this emergent language / *I love / he loves / she loves / we love* / mapped departures / on backs of school books / home country power gasp / generator conk / cold through the blocks / the students burned textbooks / goodbye Lenin-tongue / passports fallen from states / thrown stones / Rositsa stayed warm / willed an American summer / a fire at the foot of the bed / what if this isn't going to last / just *she loves* his violin / Bartók and Gershwin / scraped the sky open for her / now steel / now silver / now an ocean / now an island / drowned in lights

TO MY POLISH AUNTS

    after Allen Ginsberg

Skin pale and pocked with moles,
your names pulled from Slavic litanies,
were strong enough for farm work, had the taste
of whole milk: Bertha, Elsie, Hannah,

in your kitchens, I sat on wooden chairs,
one eye looking for the coal-grayed cats
come up from the mouse-paradise cellar, or
on the glass jars of oils and herbs—

twisted aliens floating and preserved
like the saints to whom you'd pray
to make me fatter, to cure rashes,
never a prayer for a child of your own,

or at least none answered.
In your houses, I was all brash New World—
wanting peanut butter, Dr. Pepper,
my shorts a shock of orange

against the dust and pickled wallpaper,
all American lust for plastic and the newly-made,
distaste in my mouth for the crackling
polka record, the girdles waving on the line

like Polish mother-ghosts, or the spirits
of your younger selves, the selves I couldn't see,
who spoke of love and energy in another
tongue, danced on bunion-less feet,

hair crimped with flowers. What I'd find—
long locks of waving auburn—
wrapped in tissue, after you'd all died.
Even with that bird-weight memory

in my hand, I mocked you—
your porcupine kisses, the haunted
player piano, witch herbs, deaf ears—
with a laughter that made my father frown.

Dear Aunts, the Pope is dead,
the old country prospers
tentatively after a thousand years
of tanks. Dear Aunts, we left

the Saint Joseph buried in the yard.
Forgive us our forgetting,
forgive me my blonde youth
burning like your yesterdays at the table.

Know I will be you some day—
my face will turn
as foreign as a century.
A small child will sit in my kitchen,

smelling of grass and citrus,
the food I've served untouched,
for fear she might cross
the invisible line between us.

POSTCARDS, BULGARIA

    i.

dear C—we followed a Fiat's dust
for hours the mountains repeated
in worn lines I write the same
chicken coops and onion dome
rooftops carry the weight of centuries
of what is stifled beneath
what beckons above
it reminds me of D—
at her funeral looking
up inside the copula
built in memory of
how the faces of the holy
were chipped away

ii.

C—took a cab with R to the club it was so cold
cabbie smoking shouted *American*
you hear this it came from
where you are you hear this
in your country it's bigger it's badder
your George Bush isn't afraid
to show them who's boss I had to laugh
radio beat *what goes around*
comes around the young pop star
dancing with the static violin
from another channel in the dank
cab we opened our ears looked outside
a coalition of snow and children sniffing glue

iii.

there's been another school shooting
in your country I'm sorry B woke me
the news in the hotel morning no sun yet
the airplanes still sleeping the streets
soft with snow and drunken
street dancers whirl their children
spin shoeless but they have
hats C—hats red as stars
they open their eyes see
peasant wants worker wants
grain and steel the gaping mouth is home
is a bed is a street is a lie is
a country we've been told dear C—
I'll never know but I send this anyway

HAIKUS: ROSITSA'S LUGGAGE

has been felt up by
TSA, the sausages
gone but not, *thank God*,

Tsveta's rakia
and not, by some miracle,
baby Marina's

umbilical cord:
Rositsa needs to bury
it in Harvard Yard.

No one is looking—
umbilical cords match mulch.
When Marina grows

up, she will feel this
longing, a force pulling her
to this spot. Summer.

Cambridge hot, brilliant.
A wish a baby's mother
made. A myth. Rosi

and I take the T.
We're talking about babies,
dirt under our nails.

RICKY'S BACK FROM IRAQ

What if we never left
this state? Call a tour
through the corn field, a duty
at the nursing home instead,
but won't it still end
in tattoos and diabetes, a debate
over daily bread?
Never get a bitch's name—ever.
Not even a wife
who'd promised she'd wait.
Knock on the screen door
for underage Yuenglings, then drive
to *Transcending Flesh*,
sparked-out neon, cigarette
store front.
For reasons we won't explore,
we've taken to permanence.
The girl with the silver-grip-feeler-gauge-foot-switch
is Gina. I know her from homeroom.
She's given up arms
for wings—an inferno
climbs her collarbone, reclaims
limbs. Teeth chipped like corncobs.
Says, *you look the same*, to me.
My memory holds her in white, giving
communion.
Holy Gina.
*We can make it
into a gun or something*, she tells Ricky.

Julie's name like shrapnel
in his brain.
M16. AK47.
Trigger on
the ankle bone.
S'gonna hurt like a dick, she says. *Sorry.*
Julie.
He knows there will be more in life
he can't erase. Gets a red circle
with a bar running through it,
right over her name, crossing her out.
It's funny.
The needle burns.
Might as well be honest, he says.

VALENTINE'S DAY, MANHATTAN

The bar has red lights under the chairs
(swanky) and Frank's in the hot seat,
undertaker at his father's funeral home
in Hoboken—tells us insane stories
about how sometimes they get a body
on the embalming table that's not really dead.
He says, *Once you start draining 'em
it's too late to go back.*
So it's possible to die once
and then again, at the hands of your preserver,
some guy from Jersey, who'll tell your story,
perhaps amp it up a little for shock value
at a Meat Packing District bar.
We shriek, cover dark holes in our faces
with our hands, squeal like a bunch of kids
and the undertaker eats it up.
We ignore the thoughts of your sister,
on a table in a grim basement,
the flag-draped funeral that followed, when someone like Frank
(his face flushed from too much whiskey)
had on a calm suit and an empathetic expression.
We were there in our mourning black,
and youth was nothing to be boisterous about.
None of that's real at the bar called "Tonic"
except afterward, emerging from the subway,
arm-in-arm and almost home,
we pass a bouquet of flowers,
cheap carnations chucked to the gutter
by an angry lover, and I remember

how you tossed the last flower
into your sister's grave in a field in Pennsylvania.
How you stood and watched it fall, never expecting
its restless refusal, how it would fly
from the earth, turning over itself
in the air, always landing in your hand,
needing to be buried again and again.

COMMONWEALTH

Record the map of riddled cracks
        in the cellar before the fracking starts
                beneath the school, the house. A warning

dropped casual from the mailman, the pharmacist.
        A desk drawer full of photographs, dates glowing
                in the corners like apparitions. Some

weaponry. What's that about the way they use
        the groundwater? Hasn't *commonwealth* always been
                the empire's salve? So many ways

we undermine each other.
        Such insatiable hunger,
                this coast. Should we still drink

from the tap? No one told us anything
        about a silent spring. Three Mile
                Island: a joke or a t-shirt,

the bumper stickers are not concerned
        with any of this. Just guns and their antithesis,
                the soft apostrophes of fetuses. For miles, we drove

behind *Don't like coal? Freeze in the dark,*
        yuppie scum. This, for the likes of me. The Prodigal.
                Escapee. When I sleep, don't I come back

to these fallen down streets? That cornfield
        where you put your hand to my face?
                The slag mountain's rough back

remembered in my anatomy.
        Wasn't it this ruined river that led me
                to the sea?

KOWALEWSKI vs.

Covalesky. This waiting island not yet
the destination. He'll go with the latter—
the authority of uniform,
those quick ship-spit seconds,
legs still pitching ocean-heave—
so what of spelling? The weight of paper
will outweigh what was known
as truth. Other generations choose
variations on a theme:
Coveleski. Softer with the C,
the added E. Less alien. A weaker knee.
Less Soviet fist, less brandished
rolling pin. Kovaleski
with a K, an A,
phonetic for the telemarketers,
but less compromise.
In a phone booth in Warsaw, I learn
it's Kowalewski,
as common as Smith.
Means: Iron-worker.
No wonder.
Such fire needed
to bend it. Such hot sizzle
in the plunge
into assimilation.
I'm Kowalewska here.
Ends with A for woman.
Alpha. Begin.

Outside in the snow, the Polish move
through the miracle
of reconstruction. This city once
hacked, buildings melted
and jagged, rewritten
by hate and shattered weight.
Now, it's faux-perfect.
The old town, a snow-globe,
a souvenir paperweight.
Only the ground, they say, is higher,
so the old is underneath
the broken bricks, the blown-out
glass, the people, their clothes,
and bones,
and teeth,
their occupied tongues,
their emptied ghetto,
their long history of wrongs.
Back up, the cobbles
reset by hand, by held-on
memory,
the phone box,
sort-of, steady.
I'm between
work and
sleep and work
and flight.
I find Kowalewskis,

a hundred, more, each W to lift the vowel
before.
I know this now. I'm learning
to listen better. I'm learning
to speak
my own name, no longer
tangled on my tongue.
If I tear the page,
the phonebook will dangle,
imperfect, waiting
for someone
to come looking
for another someone
in this city,
and if it's
Kowalewska,
she'll be gone.

III.

III.

ALTERNATE INVITATIONS TO A METEOR SHOWER

if we're going

there shouldn't be any light

disaster's close brush requires
another world

we want to imagine
our alternate humanness

tight swirl of possibility
star and gorgeous cloud forest,
some

building,
clear the land—
rough

an alphabet of asteroids

like waiting, open mouths
that would end it all,
this was all ruins
here, before,

to be able to see
green from the stars
(skyscrapers burned out in the distance)
fill a thermos of tea, wear sweaters—
belief in

redemption
without so many centuries
of hurt
but what if, even in this
(an)other world, a dying

colonial is
bent on nation
instructing his men to
be
with the women

they'll find
a history carved into cliffs
hitched to the sun
door frames pitched
for the one
they'll say to each other—

thank God we showed up

                                        what the scientists discuss in
this Near-Earth   Object Program
terrifies   (we can't understand)
we'll ship the last of   the obelisks from Peru to Japan
                                      sleep through
what's coming: curled in our sweaters
                                      warmed by what was once
a kingdom   for beasts

carve into the veins   of coal in a cellar
so we don't know
the difference
between night   and what we're falling through

after all   this time
we're still trusting   unreliable narratives—
                                      doubting your body's pull toward mine
                                      and if we're going to be honest
we should have   left
                                      those stones sleeping

another thousand years

AUBADE: TO EACH HIS DULCINEA

For one winter we lived
over a wedding dress shop.

Milk tea sunrise
after eight. The end

of a time zone. The end of cold
under the door. Trees restless

in their long limbs like dancers
stretching before the ballet.

Always *Don Quixote*. Always canary birdsong
from the old lady's tiled balcony.

We listened from the bed,
let the sun run

its hands over our skin.
Oranges in the trees,

peels on the bedside table
curling around the memory

of fruit. Beneath us, all that hope
on display, tried on, again and again.

LEVEL, MADAM, LEVEL.

Memory—a flurried globe. I turn us.
Even our hair stays in place. The kitchen sunlight
all night long. It was a year for making
our mothers' recipes backwards
and feeding each other with our hands.
Salt in your mouth, words in my hair.

But, no. Memory—
a peninsula of a thousand miles. We're perched
at the land's end. The confusion
of so many waves. Your voice coming through
like the trains outside Mystic, like the words we loved:
anthracite queen and *isthmus* and *terrific*.
A year without lines to color in,
so the world could become
EMU LOVE VOLUME and atomic tangerine.

We stopped taking the shortcut
behind the parking lot, between the hospital
and the cemetery. You asked
for toothpaste in the morning, maps
to hidden cities on the weekends.
The knowledge of archipelago—
that kind of lost forever, that kind of watery division.
You asked for *hello*.

Hold the mirror and let the sun hit your face
just there. The strength of it will shatter us
eventually: terracotta roofline sinking
below my feet, the waves lapping
too close, your words unending snow.
Turn us again.
I'll keep that one star in your eye,
over my shoulder, all the way down.

HALF ORANGE

This winter city loves her curves,
dresses up in oranges:
fiesta tassel trees stole
the banana girl's earrings.

Underfoot, squashed and pulpy,
a decadence of seeds
wasted on cobblestones. When the men
shake the trees in barrio Santa Cruz,

they scatter and bounce,
florescent squirrel bounty.
Oranges on the church steps, in the gutters,
like beads of paint on old photographs.

We kick one—back and forth—through the plaza,
home. Around us, couples walk arm-in-arm
for evening paseo, have a saying
used to talk about each other—
mi media naranja. My better half.

In the palace of Pedro the Cruel, I call your name,
hear my voice disappear into the jeweled dome.
They call it La Media Naranja, this vaulted heaven,
kaleidoscopic, a decked-out mistress.

You're in Pedro's gardens,
under the Traveler's Palm. For the afternoon,
I'll put my head in your lap. Forget.
Parrots do their clunky, busy soaring.

You squeeze an orange into my mouth,
skin still on. The juice: bitter,
but so bright. A stain on my cheek,
a jewel in my throat.

11:59 P.M.

La Niña, a girl Christ touching her toes
to the gulf stream, makes it snow.

Plastic cherubim lit on the neighbor's lawn
wear softer feathers. Count as they swirl

from the sky, catch them on your tongue like hosts.
Slip a little on the icy driveway, laugh

as we unlock the door. Like this we end
another year—our familiar bed, our tangled limbs.

Clank of the old radiator, the only
bells. In the morning, my kitchen stays cold,

the church empty. We have no desire
for our mothers' traditions—

pork and sauerkraut for luck against
a god-hand playing yo-yo with the planet,

a new year impossible without
the blessing of solemn gold and stone. My mother's voice,

my grandmother's singing—*praise to God,*
who lengthens out our days, who spares us yet another year.

This time we want to measure,
grasp, elongate, hold—

you and I think we can keep it
differently. I pull you closer, want to

need only your body, late-night
pizza. No otherworld.

The bed. The glowing
angels buried on the lawn.

CONFESSIONAL

    Byrnesville, PA

I want to know what you're whispering, love,
in the dark box next to mine.
We're not sure we have faith in this,
that an old priest's creaking prayers
can make us clean. With heads lighter
from fasting, we recount
how we wronged each other
all year—
    forgive me,
        you, who are deserving of all my love,
but we're so young
    these sins that weigh
will someday fade and pale like the icons
    the old women kiss.
        What deaths they're thinking of
    with so many children
grown while ours still slumber
    in our veins.
Not far from here
there's a town with your name—
it's gone, completely. Ultimatum
with steamroller megaphone. Mattress
skeleton in the weeds. Broken rings of
road, crabapple trees. Wander with me
    like these ghost families,
        our skin washed in the smoke
            of sacred palms.
    We'll never tell
what we said back there. I'll burn

my histories elsewhere—
this land not home
until I asked it to define
the differences in our beginnings.
      We'll take what we can salvage—
wood,
    wire,
        birdsong,
            crumble.
We'll banish our truths
to a lightless place, then sleep.
Then eat for days.

A PHOTO OF PENNSYLVANIA IN FIJI

after Richard Hugo

Row house with a low slung porch.
Daisy-print housedress, coal
bucket, cricket dusk, hair gray static. Always
those mountains behind you,
where riddled veins map a deep
underworld, weave our history

in hard black ink. How they bleed
across the state, Appalachian sash
on a plain beauty queen who'll never win.
With nightfall, your black-lunged husband,
football and fistfights in brotherhood bars.
The Saturday church will heave with your wishes,

coins in baskets to the heathen abroad.
Winter waiting just behind the altar's
Cyrillic promises. Where I am is winter, too—
the mountains sleep loudly, their bodies
undisturbed. Children dressed in American t-shirts
cheer a soccer match on TV.

The players' bodies twist and waver
in impossible contortions, dreamlike,
with the fitful signal. Like this we reach
to the impossible—another time, another
place—antenna outstretched
on top of a strangler fig tree.

THE OTHER SIDE OF WATER

Just what is missing in us, that needs so many worlds?
— Alan Williamson, "Sleep"

Sundays, after the toreros have thrown down
their swords and tight sunlit

jackets, we eat bull-tail for luck,
listen with our skin to the castanets' chatter,

fly a bit, over the country's bad teeth,
off the causeway and into the sea. Over and over,

we'll jump. All afternoon, if we want.
Never quite the same splash,

but always the same sand as our toes hit bottom,
the quick, hard swim toward the sun.

Once, a thousand tiny fish—
you never even felt them as they scattered.

Together again, they made a chain-mail curtain
out by the flamenco club on the pier.

You said we'd get that kind of intuition
if we could only learn to swim off the whirlpools

we create. Tap into our lateral lines.
Back on the other side, we'll remember

it differently. The fishmongers on the street corner
will open their chests, and they will be empty.

The magnolia trees bloom in August,
stand bare in May. You and I will want

to go searching again. The memory of body,
of fish in water, the way they moved

with everything, held
the light, the waves.

THERE, THERE CATASTROPHE

Byrnesville, PA

As if to show how we must weigh our suffering
        against grace—only the concrete Virgin
                remains, the ground beneath her
sunk, palms upturned, a perch
      for birds unbalanced,
              snake curled under
sandaled feet.
      Look, this quiet catastrophe—

a town gagged out,
      pāhoehoe in the country,
            buckled bread-top road,
      Graffiti Highway,
disaster toadstools,
      in the hollers—sink
holes. You and I talk of Deception

Island, of Chernobyl.
      This place, some refuge
            for a century at least, while men
fractured deep into so much sleeping
      stone for company-
store bread.
      Oh, Holy Mother upended,

bathtub Titanic—
      Virgin on a Half-Shell—
we laughed about you later
      on my grandmother's pullout sofa,

>   dug out our histories, traced
our seams—

who's to say when we'll turn
    to you, what sinking ship
        we'll inhale,
    what child-shroud.

The first warning a mystery: they said
    the cellar became a cloud,
        immigrant mothers bent
over pleats and collars—
    washed, ironed,
        breathed it in.

CENTRALIA MINE FIRE PROJECT: HISTORY
AND RECOMMENDATIONS FOR CONTROL

What is a town
worth? Once the fire reaches
the highway, then what?   State
        of panic descending. *Ask them again.*
Carbon-monoxide monitor
        malfunction. A deep and dreamless
sleep. Pressurized tankers.   Fly
ash. Not defended
        by powerful
legislators. Incompetent
rock strata. Odor of sulfur
        in the elementary
school classrooms. Night gas
alarms. Industry in reverse. The religious
        declined   to comment. Children
with unusual
headaches.   Put your name
on the monitor wait-
list. $500,000 in real
        estate. Tearing the town
apart.   Ask them again.
        Disaster
Programs Director. Live in and   endure
a police state. Last resort
        housing. Formal
Condemnation   Process.
        By the time the paramedics
got there, he had opened his eyes
        but he wasn't really   seeing.

TRIPTYCH WITH EXCERPT FROM
COAL MINER'S INDUSTRIAL HANDBOOK

There are ways to live
without memory's pull.
                What we won't talk about:
                Sunk negatives. A person
                I can't visit with again.
                                  The Babel of tongues

To keep the limbo of
motion, never rooting.
                I've torn myself
                from you before. Departures
                decked, midnight shipwreck.
                                  spoken in the mines is just

Twist the mind away
from the passed-down
markings of the body.
                What our hands did,
                to others, our tongues—
                leave me and him, leave
                                  as dangerous as on board

Right the tongue,
smooth out the accent.
Level.
                the evidence.
                                  the ship.

COAL COUNTRY, WITH ANNIVERSARY

I'm beginning to understand
    what it means to begin

when you've already ended.
    In the shadow of another year,

this slag mountain exhales.
    Never meant to be, but what happens

when you unearth for decades.
    Look, the crows dive away

and circle back—how they remember
    the buried picket of trees.

Come walk with me in the ruined
    creek. This wasteland certain

of another world.
    A fern's arm stretched

toward a kinder sun.
    Here we can break

the mountain in pieces
    with bare hands—

begin to feel each hidden silver
    unfurl. In this

shale fossil, another
    silent resurrection.

THE FLOATING ISLAND

Why is this so important? Where we come from
        and where we went—a lifetime
                of footprints, a crosshatched map,
and if we tried to plot it out wouldn't we be amazed
        at our infinite aimlessness, the ferocity
                      of our love, the heft of our regret?
What if I told you there is a floating island kingdom
        made of reeds. I swear
                the tops of our heads touched the sky,
and the people, decked in rainbow yarns
        and conch, could tell each deep blue
                stitch and gather in the water
                        as if they'd quilted the lake themselves—
        and so never got lost.
Still, their stories
        pocked with fear,
                of listless wandering.
            They lit a fire and told of a time
when a fisherman's island
        became unmoored and tugged away,
                quiet as a breath between bamboo.
When the fisherman returned
        his home was not where he left it,
                and for years his wife and child
drifted one way, and he another—
                      this lake so vast,
                          how do you save a place
in water—
        until they finally found each other.

        You asked: *what then?*
What of those silent years?
      He saw her face and thought it hadn't
          changed. Child, sun-dark, tall,
              his eyes the same. Years
of shared desire, of waiting under an indifferent
      sky had bent their hearts into different shapes—
condor,
        alpaca,
             snake.
In other words, it was too much
                time. Nothing
                    but time.

IV.

LIMBIC MORNING

If smell is the strongest sense connected
to memory, I can find you anywhere.
A city bus, wet woolen coat—
and suddenly I'm back, out of all this,
to your porch swing, lifting over summer's street,
brown bread rising in the kitchen,
mothballs in the lilies ward off rabbits.

Like this you're resurrected to my morning.
Uproot with you the long cord of your life:
Carpathian mountains, ocean cradle,
children huddled in a bed, babies you'd outlive. Wars
and winters, church bells calling up the hill—
time enough and never time enough.

That summer day I asked you, *When your husband
died, what happened then?* You said, *Good riddance,*
without looking at the child,
maybe thinking I was old enough
to glimpse the deep mine of your truths.
Summer buzzed around us. Your eyes stayed
on the mountains, and I said nothing,
breathed in mothballs, wanted lilies.

Today you're giving me another chance.
You've brought what's far beyond your grave:
vague scents of loam, your mother's country.
Dirt under nails, rose-petal rosary

between fingers. Who were you then?
You can't tell me, only whisper words
in a long-lost tongue, and in my mind I hang on
to your steady housedress, your hands
pulling cucumbers, holding a bucket, painting a fence.

ROSITSA AT THE COMMUNIST MONUMENT

Buzluzdja, Bulgaria

Half-way up the mountain, my body rebelling
with morning sickness, Rosi hung over and pissed about hiking.
Only Americans hike, she says,
and for no good reason. To admire the trees.
To get imperialistic and ready
to conquer something.
She had to ditch her stilettos and fish plastic sandals
from the trunk of the car. She's humoring me.
Hers, the generation who wants
none of this bleak memory, just
another H&M, tighter jeggings, louder folk-pop,
English-English, the sterility
of supermarkets, and more Vin Diesel, *please*.
This generation wants to turn
a defunct monument into a discotheque, a museum.
Or a discotheque museum.
There's vision there, I'll give them that. It's monstrous.
It makes you want to chase
vodka and fist pump and lose your mind and cry.
Squat on a mountaintop, built to look like a landed UFO.
We all suspected the Commies were up to this—
only in our cold terror fantasies their concrete spaceships could fly,
cross borders and oceans, drop missiles or maybe KGB
paratroopers into our cornfields.
In true communist style, you have to earn it—
hike up the side of a mountain, past Roma campfires and a boy
riding bareback and shirtless who gives us the finger and a wink.
Rosi's old enough to remember

the day the wall fell, her Russian mother crying
in a cab. The day the ice cream shop offered
flavors other than strawberry. The day she started speaking
English. The neighbor, returned from the labor
camp. Black market shuttering. A time before
refugees, cocaine, short skirts, homelessness, MADE IN CHINA, passports.
How to make sense of a country waking
if no one can agree on the dream?
Let's start here. A mountain in the middle of the country.
The monument now graffiti canvas, beautiful palimpsest, cacophony
for the clouds to wash west. Rositsa and I climb
the bombed-out rebar stairs. Over the entrance:
FORGET YOUR PAST.
Faces of communist heroes tagged
TRAITOR. A debate raging
on the south-facing flank:
FUCKUSA. BMWMAFIA.
AMERICATHEBEAUTIFUL.
We circle the thing, a beached relic, occupied
by starlings who swoop and fickle the tall grass, dart close
to our heads, return through wind-made holes
to nests they've built in the ruins. I don't go inside—
there's something corpse-like in such damp and groaning
steel and I'm in the grass, doubled over
by the future. My own ruins charred and smoldering
on another mountainside, 6000 miles behind.
It's Rosi who finds the quiet in there,
surrounded by her history,

retold in a crumbling, defaced mosaic.
She stays long enough for me to worry,
chips a piece off Marx's nose,
puts it in her pocket to take home to her mother.

LIMBO

February, my northern city
is tongue-on-a-flagpole freezing.
We go to a nude Russian spa, where Olga
tosses us some plastic slippers and will serve us borscht
in the windowless café when we're done,
our bodies soft and thawed like noodles.
But first, the wooden sauna, walls exhaling,
a eucalyptus branch for beating away
the cold, old country-style. I look at my husband and he's missing
a leg. The couple across from us—half-lost
to steam and dark. I'm beginning to think
this is what Limbo must be like.
Somewhere outside Pittsburgh
my mother is trying not to believe in it.
Pittsburgh breathes the kind of cold Steeler fans love
because it lets them wear all their black and yellow gear at once. Terrible
towel cold. But my mother won't go
to a spa, and a steam room would make her feel
like she was on MTV, and that channel
is immoral. To keep warm she'll make a pot of borscht
the way her grandmother taught her,
and my father will stoke a fire and the house
will smell like brisket and Christmas.
They'll pack up their sweaters and drive
over the mountains to make sure
my grandmothers are warm
and not missing too much
church. They won't heat the building during winter,

so the old folk sit on pews
with their heavy coats on,
an extra layer God has to peel back
to forgive their
sins like gossiping at bingo
and not taking their blood pressure medicine.
Sins, like wishing your husband with Alzheimer's
would die so he could stop not knowing
you, the children you made, the dog he loved,
stop not remembering
your honeymoon in Delaware,
where you tiptoed onto a deserted beach
and stashed your department store bathing suits
behind some rocks, ran
full tilt and laughing, your breasts bouncing,
his penis flapping up and down,
and fell into a wave, felt it smack
you on your naked stomach,
run its hands through your hair.
There was nothing between you then,
nothing but water and sunlight and the fathoms
of an ocean, cold and deep.

THE ROAD TO FETHIYE

What roils this coast—a throated call
to prayer with angelus bells, boat masts
tossed in the wake of a low pressure front,

a fight in our rental car about what
price apricots, about the stories
we tell. We are ambassadors from a land

where everyone believes they're gods
or God-fearing, where the distance between
faith and fear is measured code orange

and yards down. Even these women, shrouded
in peacock drapes, hibiscus bloom,
hijab swept cloud, will find themselves

written in. So many women here, walking
the roadside with their children,
girls in kohl and curls, boys stick-limbed

and chord-less song, babies
on their inside hips. In me, our first-born
swims, poppy seed, void

of color. Devoid of what's written.
It hears my voice,
and from the minarets, *Allāhu*

akbar. Look how we believe
what we're doing. Look how I follow
such tedious maps. I eat apricots

for iron. I count time in fingertips.
I wish I could feel more
life than heat—my hair pulled off

my neck, into your bed, a rope
around your wrist. In time, we will cut
all chords and all tethers, and I will

need to find a new way
to breathe. Over and over,
I'll face it. Along the coast, men tie up

their boats, fear their love
affair with the sea. You fear the distance
between a man in a boat and the land

he can't see anymore, and I, the distance
between weeks, how a person can grow
fingers from indistinguishable fists.

POEM WITH SO MANY BODIES IN IT

Punta de la Peña

My son wants to know more
about bodies. *Really, how did God
make the bodies. Like, the bones.
And the blood. And the water, too.*
I remember swimming in a body
of water at the feet of a fortress
adorned with stork nests.
This way—Mediterraneo.
This way—Atlantico.
They were trying to decide where one body began
       and another ended.
My son was not yet a body.
My body was younger and firmer—
it had not yet carried other bodies.
On the beach, all those beautiful
bodies laid out for sun worship.
It was almost Easter and so we waited
for a parade, waited to place our prayers under
the Virgin's embroidered robes.
A mother's body reincarnated
in ancient candle stars and papier-mâché.
The body she bore, dead,
       but resurrecting.
My son wants to know about that, too.
*What do you mean, we won't see the dead
ever again?* I swam
in an ocean that was also the sea,

try as the governing bodies might
to differentiate. That same water held
boats brimming with refugees. That same
water washed up their lone shoes
and paddles. Battered. Water-worn. Impossible
to tell to which body
they were lost. That same body
of water spat a toddler out on a beach.
   I can't bear
that story. I pour more water
into my son's cup. I tell him
Eat your dinner. I say *Adam*
and Eve. I say *Jesus*. I tell stories
and I tell lies. I bathe his body each night
in warm water, never too deep.
I return again to the beach, the small body
left there as if asleep. I think about the water,
how it held and rocked him
just like the body of his mother.
They found her body later, floating
in the water. I think about what she could have
said when he asked her
about the bodies,
the bones, the blood.
What she told him
when he asked about the water.

ROSITSA IN LOVE IN ENGLISH (ii)

What if the mop wasn't a mop,
    but a bureaucrat
        to waltz with all night,
    admire her perfect reworking of so many
diamond-soled dusty footprints helixing together
    She circled desert water round the
        Houston Marriott lobby, a glint of silver
           off mirrored letters
What if the bureaucrat gives
    a green card promise
        to the girl with the best understanding
    of Todor Zhivkov,
        Malia Obama,
           and martial arts

It's late in America now, and we're drinking
    to Rositsa's memories—
        The *Self-Defense Class for Night Workers*
           in Spanish, not English: ¡aguas aguas!
Parking lot flat snarl before daybreak
    True what they said
        about the guns,
    the political correctness,
        the biscuits
True also, the sound of danger
    Off-pitch and fueled by misplaced
        anger

Sleep all day, a chemical color
	The longed-for New York
		only a flash out the airplane window,
			staccato with steel over the wing

And at the saved-for rodeo—
	two girls, black hair streaked blue, faces painted
		with red stars,
	the whole arena crazy in love, waving flags

AT THE MALL WITH THE ANTHRACITE QUEENS

We hold our faces to a machine
and out comes a video showing who we are
with different hair. We put it in the VCR
and laugh and eat lasagna and hate ourselves
for all that cheese the way we hate
our hair no matter what. This is the middle
of Coal Country. When someone asks where
you're from you say, *hard coal*, and you are not speaking
metaphorically. At the Ukrainian festival
they will crown another Olga or Tiffany
the Anthracite Queen. She'll parade to the fairgrounds
where the Ferris wheel lights up the night,
a chandelier aflame and toppled in a ball-wrecked
house, the slag mountain skyline lit
in dollar store tiki cups floating like snow ash
above the river. On nights like these
we like to think we're living
free of theft, of malice, there is only Pennsylvania,
our lungs finally breathing
something clean and hidden, what a pick-ax
might have driven from underneath ice. Each breath not taken
at the expense of something else.
Like, say, the rocks.
Don't ask how they got in the river.
They hulk there like strangers.
Too small to build on. The kind of boulders that catch
straps on life-vests and turn them into drown-jackets.
The Anthracite Queens will go to a funeral about this.

Casket closed for bloat. The Anthracite Queens sing
in the choir. They love to sing and they love to research
genealogy. They want to discover
their grandmother's name, see her passage,
claim their own Plymouth Rock.
Some of the Anthracite Queens remember
how the grandmothers were carried here:
in the arms of a ship,
in the arms of their mothers, in the arms
of flight, but also choice and free will.
Some of the Anthracite Queens
forget this. When the demagogue flies in
and calls their state
capital *war zone* they feel the burn
of shame. The news shows another row house
like a face on fire, eyelash flames
and white vinyl melting
and black men on the street meant to look like rocks
in a river. *How can we trace*
this fire? Everyone wants to know.
Hurry up and ask already then.
Before the well slugs dry again.
Before someone gets deployed.
Before someone gets fired. But maybe
the Anthracite Queens already know? They have to have
seen this coming. They are outside
but they are not outsiders. The machine
shows them how to be anything it imagines:

The Party Girl,
           The Business Lady,
                      The Clean
Cut, The Cutie Pie, The Lady
           Who Lunches, The Punk Rock, The All American
                      Girl.
After all, this was supposed to be
the final resting ground, the end
of scrabbling, of stripping, of searching, a kingdom
of light built on rock,
or, depending on how the sun hits,
a city aflame and fractured
on long gone impossible beasts.

ROSITSA IN LOVE IN ENGLISH (iii)

or The Tale of the Martenitsa

Shake your mattress one last time.
        Feathers in the air like late spring snow.

All the trees in town hum a red and white love
        story. All the girls tie their hopes

to the trees. First hint of petals on a wet black
        road that leads to the embassy or the interior.

Which way will you go today?
        Free to roam, but the borders will be

hard black water and a lost lottery.
        At the bus depot, green lip hyacinth,

bucketful of narcissus, country gold
        sold by babushkas.

What kind of year will this be?
        Myth will make you look under

a rock. Luck will tell you to never
        take it off.

Faith will invite him
        back to your bed.

The babushka strokes your smooth cheek
>   when she sells you a fistful of daffodils.

Hope loses your charm
>   in the road, but keeps you walking anyway.

IF YOU WONDER WHY THE RIVER

In front of the sinking
Ukrainian Club, an old Veteran
plays an accordion—reedy, old world,
before-the-cold-war, after-the-rapture tune.
My cousin and I drive late night to drink
Yuengling. We are out-of-state
license plates, white teeth and tanned shoulders,
and this is not our mother's country
anymore. When you ask them,
they'll tell you about the Coney,
the Italian wedding band, and we see 1950,
demand poodle skirts. Even as close
as we are, we still just want costumes.
      If you wonder why the river
runs orange, no one will tell you.
When you ask who paid for the broken
arm, they say potatoes. We know
the living room where he had his last heart
attack, but we'll never go inside.
Of course, the town got leveled.
Yes, the fire's still going.
Yes, they left the old country for this.
No, we can no longer speak
their language. If you want to find
your father, he's not
underground anymore. He's up there,
building windmills.

A WEDDING IN POLAND

After so much vodka, all communist blocks
    look the same. I'm calling up tapped intercoms,
        repeating a name. Sunrise. No one on the other end

anymore—shipyards gone rusted,
    stock market's sailing and our bride's about to fly
        off to Boston. We throw a confetti of copper

pennies at her feet, wishing her
    children. All the guests wild
        with benevolence, Luksusowa,

gosh-ko gosh-ko gosh-ko gosh-ko!
    and someone bring out the eels already.
        We toss salt over our shoulders.

The leader of the band plays the dollar dance perfection—
    uncles paper the bride from white
        to green. Dawn, and it's still the same day,

won't rest until noon, wake for dusk and change
    into our boldest reds, a dance-
        floor of poppies swirling.

All that symbolism, all that myth, and so another round
    rips from the Ukrainian saxophonist,
        who screams out his homeland as the sun sets

again—
    we'll all
        chant with him as we spin:

No borders
    No borders
        No borders

WHATEVER WE NAME, WE EXCEED

Or in the naming, lose
our power. I called you
house and light and pushed you forth—

with each new month
you show me I was wrong:
Here, you've made a house with bones
of cloud. Look now, your darkness is
so bright. Of course,

you're right—
I call this love. It burns to ash,
and—never bird—returns
to flame.

When the border fell and armies
came, they cut not only arms but tongues.
They opened every house
and muted ears, and when the family

landed on these once again rebranded shores
they found the rocks weren't rocks,
the bread not bread,
the letters broken, hammer-scattered,
the sky a thing that hung
too low upon their heads.

Perhaps that's how I know it,
in this language their own
children would refuse—
dziecko, kochanek, matka, dzień—

these things I try to name each day
were never mine to lose.

VOLCANO WITH CHILD

I climbed in there once, the sleeping mountain
warm from within and exhaling
through invisible fissures under my sandals.
And the once-buried, now-excavated city,
the blown-out houses and casts of screaming
women, their bodies curled, their mouths
full of ash. All of it ancient
history. So long the sky,
a lemon-washed blue.
No fear, nor empathy,
perhaps a faint hunger
for the sea, a desire to dive
off the prow of a ferry or lip
of a cliff. Get sand in my teeth.
Remember the untethered
freedom of this? The privilege. Today, cloaked white
      all around, distant spring and cold
wind bothering the blossoms. Routine
steady as daybreak. I will try
to feed a child and not hear
about how others were killed but first
tortured somewhere far away from here.
But not—oceans are no longer
a distance. Continents Pangea-ed
by the miracle of flight and the knowledge
of mothering. A dark well. Ferocious
positioning of love and the promise
of disaster. Bad news lights up the phone like a false lover,

first thing awake, and then my son,
his tiptoe to my bedside, his small hand on my pregnant body.
The trees give in to a tentative green. Won't turn
course again, inevitable summer. *This is what you've become,
and that's probably going to be that.*
Luck would have it. At the end of a forgettable
season, I'll watch the sun set beyond
rooftops and the crisscross of power
lines. I'm walking home, son running ahead,
and nothing to fear: cars all parked,
his hair a spark, a flame, and he's going up the walk now,
to a house that's gray, and settled, and waiting
for us all to return with our noise and need,
like homes everywhere hope to do.

THANKS

I am so grateful for the guidance and knowledge of many people at Emerson College, especially John Skoyles, John Trimbur, Richard Hoffman and Christine Casson. For the gifts of time, encouragement and insight, I am indebted to the Squaw Valley Writers Community and to the Colrain Poetry Manuscript Conference, and would like to give special thanks to Joan Houlihan and Stephen Motika. Thank you to Curtis Perdue, Linwood Rumney, Sarah Sweeney, and Jennifer Sweeney, for their vision, advice and support as this manuscript took shape, and to Devin Kelly, Jill McDonough, and John Skoyles for their generous consideration of it. And thanks to Ron Spalletta, Anne Champion, Matt Summers, Amanda Jimenez Alley and Kristen Hoggatt, for their critique and belief in these poems.

To the people I've met on my travels and the families who welcomed me into their homes, especially Rosi Vitanova and Bobby Milkov, thank you for your stories and your friendship. I would like to extend my love and gratitude to my family, most importantly to my parents, for literally everything. To MamMam, and all the people who ever sat around her table in Shamokin and shared their stories, thank you. And to Corey, my husband—thank you for traveling this world with me, and for putting the kids to bed (again) so I can write.

For their guidance and vision, I would like to thank Michelle and Peter at Platypus Press, who put so much care into bringing this book into the world. Finally, all my gratitude to Claudia Emerson, who showed me what a poem was, and taught me that I could write one. I miss you, as all the world here misses you.

ACKNOWLEDGEMENTS & NOTES

Thanks to the editors of the following journals in which these poems first appeared, sometimes in earlier versions or with different titles: *Amethyst Arsenic*, *Bayou*, *Borderlands: Texas Poetry Review*, *Bosphorus Art Project Quarterly*, *Cimarron Review*, *Four Way Review*, *Guernica*, *The Hampden-Sydney Poetry Review*, *Hawai'i Pacific Review*, *inter|rupture*, *The Literary Bohemian*, *Meeting House*, *Minnetonka Review*, *[PANK]*, *Poets & Artists*, *Salamander*, *Split Rock Review*, and *Sugar House Review*.

"St Edith of Centralia" alludes to Wisława Szymborska's "Lot's Wife," and "Of Course She Looked Back," by Natalie Diaz.

The *"the doors"* refrain in "Porch Talk," is taken from a pre-Nicene Creed chant performed during Ukrainian Catholic mass.

The passage *"praise to God, / who lengthens out our days, who spares us yet another year."* used in "11:59 p.m.," is taken from the hymn "Wisdom ascribe, and might and praise."

"Centralia Mine Fire Project: History and Recommendations for Control" is an erasure from the book *Fire Underground: The Ongoing Tragedy of the Centralia Mine Fire* by David DeKok.

The third layer of "Triptych with Excerpt from Coal Miner's Industrial Handbook" is taken from an industrial handbook entitled *Coal-Mine Workers and Their Industry*.

"Whatever We Name, We Exceed" borrows its title from the Eleanor Rand Wilner poem "Interview."

ABOUT THE AUTHOR

Mary Kovaleski Byrnes' poems have appeared in *Guernica*, *[PANK]*, *Sugar House Review*, *Cimarron Review*, *The Hampden-Sydney Poetry Review*, *Best of Kore Press*, *Best of the Net*, and elsewhere. She is co-founder of the EmersonWRITES program, a free writing program for Boston Public School students at Emerson College where she is a faculty member in the Writing, Literature & Publishing department. Originally from Pennsylvania, she now lives north of Boston with her husband and two young children.

Please check the Platypus Press website for further releases.

platypuspress.co.uk